Love's Spectrum: Bliss to Heartache

MATLOTLO SEJAKE

Published by MATLOTLO SEJAKE, 2024.

While every precaution has been taken in the preparation of this book, the publisher assumes no responsibility for errors or omissions, or for damages resulting from the use of the information contained herein.

LOVE'S SPECTRUM: BLISS TO HEARTACHE

First edition. July 10, 2024.

Copyright © 2024 MATLOTLO SEJAKE.

ISBN: 979-8224806843

Written by MATLOTLO SEJAKE.

Table of Contents

I CHOOSE HER	1
MY TRUST	2
TWO LITTLE BIRDS	3
THE WOMEN OF MINE	4
MY LOVE FOR ALL SEASONS	5
A LOVE OF GOLD	6
MY DREAM LOVE	7
AN APPLE OF MY EYE	8
YOU ARE MY ONLY ONE	9
A LOVE THAT LASTS FOREVER	10
I WILL NEVER LIE	11
WOULD YOU LOVE ME	12
FROM BOTTOM OF MY HEART	14
WOUNDED LOVE	15
THE SWEETEST THING	16
A LOVE LIKE NO OTHER	17
IN YOUR EYES	18
WOULD YOU MARRY ME	19
ENDLESS DEVOTION	20
WE WILL NEVER BE REAL UNTIL WE MEANT TO	21
PLEASE REMEMBER	22
I DON'T CARE	23
WE WILL ALWAYS BE THE SAME	24
DON'T FORGET	25
I UNDERSTANT	26
I TRY TO LOVE YOU	27
I'M SORRY	28
LET ME TELL YOU	29

YOU'RE MY HOPE 30
A KISS OF FATE 31
HER TOUCH 32
IN MY MIND 33
A WOMAN OF INTENTIONS 34
MY REFLECTION 35
I WANT TO SAY YOUR NAME 36
MAYBE I SHOULD LET YOU KNOW 37
MY CRUSH 38
MOMENT IN TIME 39
I WILL TAKE YOU FAR AWAY 40
DISTANCE RELATIONSHIP 41
WE ARE MEANT TO BE 42
I AM 43
DO NOT BE LED BY FEAR 44
EMBRACE THE LIGHT 45
FAKE LOVE 46
REFLECTIONS OF REGRET 47
TO MY EXES 48
THE HEALING POWER OF LOVE 49
LONELINESS 50
REFLECTIONS OF MATURITY 52
TRUST IN TRANSITION 53
ECHOES OF TIME 54
WOULD YOU LOVE ME | NAKED? 55
FAMILY HUSTLE 56
SOUL'S RESONANCE 57
PROMISE OF LOVE 58
ALONE IN THOUGHT 59
LET'S BE FRIENDS 60
THE STRANGER 61

IMPERFECTLY PERFECT 62
DEAR HAPPINESS 63
MY BEAUTIFUL MIND 64
FADED LOVE... 65
LOST LOVE AT 3 AM 66
YOURS FOREVER... 67
LET YOUR MAN LOVE YOU 68
INNER STRUGGLE 69
DEAR MOM... 70
LOVE YOUR GIRL.. 71
FOREVER IN 24 HOURS.. 72
LOST IN THE DREAM 73
THE WORLD MUST KNOW....................................... 74
SELF-REFLECTION 75
BEAUTY UNMATCHED 76
STRUGGLING WITH LOVE 77
IN THE QUIET OF NIHGT 78
UNSPOKEN SECRETS... 80
THE CHANGING WORLD... 81
THE STRENGTH OF THE FAMILY 82
THE DIFFICULT ROAD OF LOVE 83
ENCOUNTER 84
NEVER BEG FOR LOVE 85
RENEWAL.. 86
DREAM OF A KISS 87
A HEART'S GRATITUDE... 88
THE BOND THAT ENDURES 89
OCEAN SERENITY...90

I CHOOSE HER

In the vast sea of faces, I choose her
    For the purpose, for the reasons, for the love she brings
    Her voice a whispered melody, her touch a gentle breeze
    I choose her for the joy she scatters in my soul
    In the quiet moments, I choose her
    For the trust she builds, for the strength she shows
    Her eyes a window to her thoughts, her smile a beacon of light
    I choose her for the peace she brings me
    In the stormy nights, I choose her
    For her loyalty, for her unwavering faith
    Her presence a shield, her words a soothing balm
    I choose her for the safety she provides
    In the brightest days, I choose her
    For how she cares, for the love she nurtures
    Her laughter a symphony, her kindness a guiding star
    I choose her for the happiness she gives me
    In the depths of my heart, I choose her
    For the bond we share, for the connection we hold
    Her essence intertwined with me, her spirit a part of me
    I choose her for the love that blooms between us
    In the journey of life, I choose her

MY TRUST

In a world where truth is absent
    And people fail each other
    Where love seems like a myth
    And fake smiles cover pain
    Where money holds more value than life
    You, my trust, my hope, my light
    Defy the odds and prove them all wrong
    The one I hold dear in my heart
    The one who never lets me down
    Oh, how I shudder at the thought
    Of a life without your guiding presence
    Perhaps a world of horror and strife
    Where everyone's an enemy
    But with you, my trust, by my side
    I find solace, strength, and peace
    A beacon of love in a world of darkness
    You're my trust, my world, my everything

TWO LITTLE BIRDS

Two little birds, always together
    Love so willingly, we're birds of the feather
    Never willingly apart, we stick close
    Even when we fly afar for work, we're quick to repose
    Oh my love, do you think of me when you're out?
    I feel lonely, without a doubt
    Your shade is the only one that cools my soul
    Always together, always making me whole
    Like two little birds, we are meant to be
    Always together, always happy, just like you and me

THE WOMEN OF MINE

In the arms of the women of mine
    I find my loving peace divine
    She molds me into the man I should be
    Her unwavering support sets my spirit free
    Oh, my dear, where else could I find
    Such an amazing love so kind?
    Your endless support knows no end
    Creating a bond that will never bend
    Together we walk the path of success
    Our love a never-ending caress
    In your arms, I find my heaven
    With you, my love, my heart is leaven

MY LOVE FOR ALL SEASONS

In the season of sunshine or snow
    You're my love for all seasons, this I know
    Through thick and thin, in all kinds of weather
    You stand by me, we face it together
    In summer's heat or winter's chill
    Your love remains constant, never still
    In times of plenty or times of strife
    You're my rock, my love, my life
    In rainy days or droughts severe
    You're the one who's always near
    You hold my hand, you dry my tears
    You calm my tears and quell my fears
    So here's to you, my love so true
    For all the seasons, I'm grateful to you
    With you by my side, I can brave any storm
    You're my love for all seasons, forever warm

A LOVE OF GOLD

In your eyes, I see a love of gold
    A beauty that cannot be bought or sold
    With you, my confidence soars high
    Your presence, like a precious gem, is my sky
    Your movements speak louder than words
    The truth in your actions, like melodious birds
    In your embrace, I find my peace
    A love of gold, never to cease
    A love so rare, like a treasure untold
    With you, my heart is forever bold
    In each glance and each touch
    I find in you, a love that means so much
    A love of gold, pure and true
    In your arms, I know I've found my due
    Forever grateful for the love we hold
    A love of gold, worth more than any gold.

MY DREAM LOVE

In the shadows of my thoughts
    Where dreams and reality intertwine
    I found the love of my dream
    A love so pure, so divine
    Through the darkness of the night
    In the jungle of my mind
    I searched and I sought
    For the love I longed to find
    And there, in the moonlit glow
    I saw your face, so clear
    My dream love, my soulmate
    Whispering sweet nothings in my ear
    In your embrace, I found solace
    In your eyes, I found peace
    My dream love, my darling
    You are the missing piece
    So let us dance in the moonlight
    And let our love ignite
    For in your arms, my dream love
    I found my guiding light

AN APPLE OF MY EYE

The fruit so red
    That sparkles so bright
    Sits in my palm
    And fills me with delight
    It's an apple
    So round and so true
    Its beauty so pure
    It steals my heart anew
    Its skin so smooth
    Its flesh so sweet
    It makes my heart sing
    With love so complete
    An apple so perfect
    From stem to its core
    It fills me with joy
    And so much more
    This little red apple
    So precious and true
    It holds all my love
    Just for you

YOU ARE MY ONLY ONE

You are my only one
    The love I hold so true
    You're the light in my life
    That shines so bright and new
    The one who makes me smile
    The one who fills my heart
    With joy and happiness
    That never will depart
    A love so deep and strong
    That's here to stay
    My only one, my love
    My everything, always

A LOVE THAT LASTS FOREVER

Two hearts
    Entwined as one
    Each beat
    A love song sung
    Two souls
    Connected deep
    A love that lasts
    Beyond sleep
    Two minds
    In perfect sync
    Their thoughts
    Each love's link
    Two lives
    Joined hand in hand
    Their future
    A golden strand
    The love of two people
    A bond so strong
    A love that lasts
    Forever long

I WILL NEVER LIE

My love is true and honest
 I'll never tell a lie
 For my heart is pure and faithful
 My feelings will not die
 I'll always be sincere
 My love is ever-true
 I'll never break your trust
 For my heart belongs to you
 No matter what may come
 No matter what may pass
 My love will always be
 A love that will last
 I'll be by your side
 My love will never cease
 I'll never tell a lie
 For you, I'll never cease

WOULD YOU LOVE ME

Would you love me
    In the light of day
    When shadows fade
    And fears are at bay?
    Would you love me
    In the darkest night
    When all seems lost
    And there's no guiding light?
    Would you love me
    Through joy and through pain
    Through sunshine and storm
    Through loss and through gain?
    Would you love me
    With all of my flaws
    With all of my scars
    With all of my raw?
    Would you love me
    With a heart so true
    With a love so deep
    That it will always renew?
    Would you love me
    As I am meant to be
    With all my faults
    With all of me?
    Would you love me
    For eternity
    With a love so pure

That it sets us free?

FROM BOTTOM OF MY HEART

From the bottom of my heart, my love for thee
    Flows like a river, vast and deep
    In every beat, in every breath
    I feel your presence, even in death
    Your touch ignites a fire within
    A passion that burns, again and again
    No words can truly express
    The depth of love I feel, I must confess
    So from the depths of my soul
    I send these words, the ultimate goal
    To show you how much you mean to me
    From the bottom of my heart, eternally

WOUNDED LOVE

In the depths of wounded love, we find
    A heart that bleeds with every beat
    A soul that aches with every breath
    Through the tears and broken dreams
    We search for solace in the pain
    But love's wounds run deep and true
    We bear the scars of love gone wrong
    And carry them like heavy burdens
    Yet still we long for love's sweet song
    In the quiet moments of despair
    We find the strength to carry on
    For in the wounded love, we find repair
    So let wounds of love inspire
    And let the scars remind us of
    The power of love's enduring fire.

THE SWEETEST THING

In your eyes, I see the sky
    So pure and full of light
    A love that's like a lullaby
    You're the sweetest thing in sight
    Your heart, a gift so rare and true
    A treasure shinning bright
    With every beat, it hums for you
    You're my guiding light
    In the chaos of the world we know
    You're the calm in the storm
    With you, my love, I'll always grow
    You're the sweetest form
    The sweetest thing in life I've found
    Is you, my love, my dear
    With you, my heart is safe and sound
    You're the sweetest thing, I fear

A LOVE LIKE NO OTHER

In a world filled with fleeting glances
    I found a love like no other
    A bond so deep, it defies all chances
    A love that only grows stronger
    With every beat of my heart
    I feel you by my side
    Never shall we drift apart
    In you, my love abides
    Through stormy seas and darkness night
    Your love is my guiding light
    A beacon that shines so bright
    In your arms, everything feels right
    A love like no other, so pure and true
    Forever I'll cherish, forever I pursue
    For in your love, I found my refuge
    A love like no other, eternally renewed

IN YOUR EYES

In your eyes, I see the world unfold
    A universe of secrets, stories untold
    The shimmering depths, like the ocean wide
    Reflecting the light, of the starry sky
    In your eyes, I find my true place
    A heaven of love, a sacred space
    I lose myself in the warmth I find
    A flame of passion, burning in your mind
    In your eyes, I see the storms rage
    The pain, the sorrow, the battles we wage
    But in the depths, there lies a peace
    A silent strength, that will never cease
    In your eyes, I see the future ahead
    A journey of joy, of tears shed
    Hand in hand, we'll face the unknown
    Together, we'll stand, united and strong
    In your eyes, I see my reflection
    A mirror of love, a connection
    In your eyes, I find my true self
    In your eyes, I find wealth
    So hold me close, never let me go
    In your eyes, I find my home

WOULD YOU MARRY ME

Would you marry me?
    My dearest love
    Would you say yes?
    Under the stars above
    Let's join our hearts
    Let's join our hands
    And share our lives
    Together, as planned
    Let's build our dreams
    Let's make them real
    With love and trust
    And a love that's sealed
    So, would you marry me
    My dearest love
    And make me the happiest
    Beneath the stars above?

ENDLESS DEVOTION

Endless devotion, a flame that never dies
    In the depths of my heart, it truly lies
    Through trials and tribulations, it still survives
    A love so strong, it never denies
    Forever bound, our souls in ties
    Endless devotion, under the starry skies

WE WILL NEVER BE REAL UNTIL WE MEANT TO

In the depths of our hearts, we search for truth
    Yearning for connection, seeking proof
    But we will never be real until we meant to
    Embracing our flaws and letting love break through
    In the shadows of doubt, we hide our fears
    Afraid to love, afraid of tears
    But we will never be real until we meant to
    Letting go of past and embracing the new
    So let us be vulnerable, let us be free
    Let love guide us, let love be the key
    For we will never be real until we meant to
    Transforming our souls and finding what is true

PLEASE REMEMBER

Please remember, dear, our solemn vow
    With gold rings gleaming on our fingers now
    In front of all, our hearts did freely confess
    That we would journey on, together, no less
    Through trials and triumphs, side by side we stand
    Bound by promises, and love's tender hand
    For only death can dare to part us two
    Our empire build on dreams, and love so true
    So hold these words close, let them never fade
    Our future paved in gold, with love displayed
    Together we'll conquer, through highs and lows
    Our journey of love, only death knows

I DON'T CARE

I don't care what others may say
    As long as you're with me each day
    Your words of support light my way
    Guiding me to the moon, come what may
    Their thoughts and opinions matter not
    For in you, I've found all I've sought
    My dreams and ambitions intertwined with yours
    Together we open new doors
    I don't care for their judgments of our love
    For our bond was formed from above
    No one can tear us apart
    For you hold the key to my heart

WE WILL ALWAYS BE THE SAME

We will always be the same
    Through sunshine and through rain
    Our love will forever remain
    In every trial we face
    In every challenging race
    Our bond will never be erased
    Hand in hand we'll walk
    With every heartfelt talk
    Together, we'll always be the same

DON'T FORGET

Don't forget, you, my happiness
    I just say it before
    I would forever be with you
    In the time of rainy season
    And the time of drought
    Do you know how much I feel when you're not feeling well?
    I'm just like nothing to compare to
    Perhaps a little drop
    Pouring on dry soil
    Don't change the contents
    Of this love we've found
    Let it grow and flourish
    In the stormy skies
    And the barren ground

I UNDERSTANT

In silence I wait, for a response
    My heart heavy with each passing day
    Understanding your choice, I accept
    But the ache of rejection does stay
    In the quiet moments, I reflect
    On the bond we once shared so strong
    Why did you choose me as your confidant
    Only to push me away for so long?
    I understand, I truly do
    That we may not be meant to be
    But the pain of being cast aside
    Will always linger inside of me
    So I will move on, with grace and strength
    And wish you well on your path
    For I understand, in the end
    It's not about us, but about our aftermath

I TRY TO LOVE YOU

In the depth of my heart, I try to love you
    But your indifference leaves me feeling blue
    I offer my love, but you refuse to see it through
    I reach out my hand, hoping you'll take it
    But you turn away, leaving my heart to ache
    I try to understand, but the pain is too great
    I long for your touch, your words of affection
    But all I receive is cold rejection
    I try to love you, but it's a one-sided connection
    So I hold onto hope, that one day you'll see
    The love I have for you, how much you mean to me
    I try to love you, even when you can't love me

I'M SORRY

In the depths of my soul, I feel regret
    For I have let you down, my dear, and I fret
    I'm sorry for the pain I've caused, I vow
    To make amends, somehow, someway, now
    Please forgive me, for I know not what to do
    But to offer my heart, honest and true
    I'll do my best to make things right
    For I cannot bear to see you in such a plight
    I'm sorry for the hurt, I'm sorry for the tears
    I promise to make it up, to calm your fears
    I'll strive to be better, to show you I care
    I'll be there for you, always, I swear
    So forgive me, my love, for I want you to see
    That I am truly sorry, for letting you down, me
    I'll make it right, I'll make it all okay
    I'll be there for you, come what may

LET ME TELL YOU

Let me tell you, my dear
    The thoughts that filled my mind
    On that beautiful day we shared together
    Only sleep was all I could find
    Let me tell you, my love
    I didn't think much that day
    But how could I sleep without a single kiss
    The memory of your lips, in my mind they did stay.

YOU'RE MY HOPE

In the darkness of my despair, you're my hope
    With you by my side, I can believe
    You listen to my words, understand my voice
    Even when secrets weigh heavy on my heart
    You never pretend, you protect
    Building something beautiful together, the best choice I've made

A KISS OF FATE

In the dance of life, we find a kiss of fate
    A meeting foretold, a bond innate
    With intertwining paths and twirling twine
    Two souls collide, in destiny's design
    A whisper on the wind, a touch so light
    A moment frozen, hearts take flight
    In shadows deep or skies so clear
    Then kiss of fate draws near, so near
    And as the stars align above
    The touch of destiny, a gift of love
    In that fleeting moment, time stands still
    A kiss of fate, a divine thrill
    Embracing what was always meant to be
    Two hearts entwined, forever free
    In the tapestry of time and space
    A kiss of fate, an eternal embrace

HER TOUCH

In the gentle caress of her touch
    I find solace and love so much
    Her fingertips like feathers, light and soft
    Stirring emotions deep and aloft
    Each brush against my skin
    Awakens feelings from within
    A warmth and comfort that I crave
    In her touch, I find my save
    Oh, how her touch can heal
    All the wounds that I conceal
    In her hands, I find my peace
    Her touch, a sweet release

IN MY MIND

In the course of my mind
    You hold me tight
    I never lie
    Crazy thoughts come, I can't deny
    Without your picture
    Without your smile
    What could I think of?
    What can smile do to nothing?
    My mind holds on

A WOMAN OF INTENTIONS

In the depths of my soul, I'm not quite sure
    What kind of man I could truly be
    Because you have shown the world my weaknesses
    Exposed my faults, my vulnerabilities
    You, untrustworthy, a women of intentions
    Stealing what is not yours, sowing deception
    Yet you demand to be treated with respect
    As if you deserve love and affection
    But I see through your façade, your charade
    Your selfish desires laid bare, displayed
    I will not be swayed by your false charm
    For I know the truth, you mean me harm
    I will stand strong, I will not be swayed
    By your deceitful game you have played
    I will rise above, a man of integrity
    No longer under your false identity
    I will find my true self, my worth
    And leave behind the shadows of your curse
    I will be the man I am meant to be
    Free from your chains, finally set free.

MY REFLECTION

In the mirror
    A reflection stares
    A perfect image
    That's not quite there
    A vision of beauty
    So clear and bright
    But in my heart
    It doesn't feel quite right
    The image in the glass
    So flawless, so real
    But inside
    A question I still feel
    Is this really me?
    I ask with doubt
    Or just a pretty face
    A false image, no doubt?
    A reflection
    So lovely to see
    But the truth within
    Is what sets me free

I WANT TO SAY YOUR NAME

In whispers soft and tender
    I want to say your name
    With each syllable well-spelled
    For the world to hear the same
    No matter where I am
    In flight or on ocean ship
    Your name is stored in my mind
    Like money numbers, I won't let slip
    Together or apart
    I won't forget the memories we made
    The way we used to be
    In this world we bravely wade

MAYBE I SHOULD LET YOU KNOW

Maybe I will let you know
    You will forgive me, I hope
    Maybe I will make you understand
    You will digest it, in the end
    Maybe I will tell you this secret
    You will show up on me, I trust
    How could I fear to tell you?
    This secret so true and deep
    Why shouldn't I be true?
    For all we've come across and keep
    Oh, my dear, please forgive me
    To you, I should build trust and see
    To tell what seats in my mind
    And leave our doubts behind

MY CRUSH

In the depths of my heart, a secret I hold
    For you, my crush, with hair of gold
    I dream of the day you'll finally see
    The love I hide so silently
    For you're the one my soul longs to hold

MY REFLECTION

In the mirror
    A reflection stares
    A perfect image
    That's not quite there
    A vision of beauty
    So clear and bright
    But in my heart
    It doesn't feel quite right
    The image in the glass
    So flawless, so real
    But inside
    A question I still feel
    Is this really me?
    I ask with doubt
    Or just a pretty face
    A false image, no doubt?
    A reflection
    So lovely to see
    But the truth within
    Is what sets me free

I WANT TO SAY YOUR NAME

In whispers soft and tender
    I want to say your name
    With each syllable well-spelled
    For the world to hear the same
    No matter where I am
    In flight or on ocean ship
    Your name is stored in my mind
    Like money numbers, I won't let slip
    Together or apart
    I won't forget the memories we made
    The way we used to be
    In this world we bravely wade

MAYBE I SHOULD LET YOU KNOW

Maybe I will let you know
    You will forgive me, I hope
    Maybe I will make you understand
    You will digest it, in the end
    Maybe I will tell you this secret
    You will show up on me, I trust
    How could I fear to tell you?
    This secret so true and deep
    Why shouldn't I be true?
    For all we've come across and keep
    Oh, my dear, please forgive me
    To you, I should build trust and see
    To tell what seats in my mind
    And leave our doubts behind

MY CRUSH

In the depths of my heart, a secret I hold
    For you, my crush, with hair of gold
    I dream of the day you'll finally see
    The love I hide so silently
    For you're the one my soul longs to hold

MOMENT IN TIME

In a moment in time
    My thoughts go wild
    Thinking of that day
    When I held you close
    Touched your breast so slowly
    I can't stop thinking
    Of my first kiss
    Like how I felt
    A rush of emotions
    A wave of bliss
    In that fleeting moment
    Time stood still
    The world faded away
    And it was just you and I
    Lost in our own little world
    Where love reigned supreme
    And our hearts beat as one

I WILL TAKE YOU FAR AWAY

I will take you far away
    To a place that deserves us alone
    Where we will always be on honeymoon
    You, my love
    From nations that don't understand our language
    We will speak it to each other along
    In this special sanctuary we'll cherish and relish
    Our bond growing ever strong

DISTANCE RELATIONSHIP

In two different worlds we reside
    Connected only by love's tide
    Across oceans, miles apart
    Yet you're always in my heart
    Through the distance, we will find
    Our love transcends space and time

WE ARE MEANT TO BE

In the sky of endless possibility
    We are meant to be, you and me
    Two birds of alpha, soaring high
    Two stones that talk, when not seen by eye
    Speaking in a language only we can understand
    A bond that can never be thrown away or banned
    For we are meant to be, like a tide to the shore
    Forever and always, together we will explore

I AM

I am the man of his choice
    I am
    A man who can choose and reject
    I am
    One man mission
    I can
    Choose what is beautiful from dust
    I can
    Have a love that I want to
    In the realm of choice, I stand tall
    My heart, my compass to guide
    With strength and wisdom, I answer the call
    In love, I'll always abide
    I am the master of own fate
    With courage, I face the unknown
    I choose my path, no need to hesitate
    In my heart, true love is shown

DO NOT BE LED BY FEAR

Do not be let by fear
    Do not bow to threats
    For love does exist
    But only when we learn to see
    The true meaning of it
    Do not fall for the unknown
    Regret is not a path we wish to own

EMBRACE THE LIGHT

Do not be swayed by fear's might
    Nor by threats that draw near flight
    Love does exist, do not doubt
    True love's worth is what love's about
    Learn its lessons, feel its mind
    Do not fall for what's not kind
    Regret is a heavy burden to bear
    So tread with caution, handle with care

FAKE LOVE

I always wonder
    Who gets into you
    Getting into your cold arms
    Getting involved with your false face
    I always wonder
    Is it me in this fake love?
    How did it start
    Proposing fake promises
    Lost in a maze of deceit
    Caught in a web of lies
    I yearn for the truth
    But all I find are empty cries
    I search for authenticity
    In a world of artifice
    Yearning for connection
    In a love that feels like a kiss
    But your words are hollow
    And your actions are lies
    In this false love I drown
    In a sea of compromise
    I always wonder
    Who gets into you
    But I know deep down
    It's time to bid adieu

REFLECTIONS OF REGRET

There will come a time
    When you'll remember me
    Day and night
    Thinking of my true self
    There will come a time
    When you'll try to call me
    But it will be too late
    There will come a time
    When you'll dream of my voice
    But know you won't hear it again
    Because you chose to leave me behind
    For another man without a reason
    And when that time comes
    I hope you finally realize
    The love and care I gave
    Was more than you'll ever find
    In another's arms
    So let that time be a lesson
    To cherish what you have
    Before it slips away
    And you're left with regret
    For the choices you made

TO MY EXES

Let me thank you
    For the lessons learned
    From our time together
    I grew stronger, wiser
    And now understand
    That love is not easy
    But it's worth fight
    Through heartbreak and tears
    I found my true self
    And learned that cheating
    Only breaks us apart
    So thank you, dear exes
    For shaping me into who I am today

THE HEALING POWER OF LOVE

Love is a balm
    To soothe the wounded soul
    A force that lifts the spirit
    To heights beyond control
    It shades the flaws and faults
    And sees the best in all
    Loving not for what one is
    But for who they are, beyond all
    The tears that stream in sorrow
    Are gently wiped away
    By hands that hold compassion
    And love that warms the day
    The smile that graces lips
    Is but a fraction of the joy
    That love brings to the heart
    And makes life worth a try

LONELINESS

Out in the world, surrounded by strangers
    I feel a sense of loneliness, a sense of danger
    I long for your company, your familiar touch
    But you are miles away, I miss you so much
    At work, you are busy, focused on the job
    Leaving me feeling isolated, feeling robbed
    Of precious moments together, of laughter and fun
    I count down the hours until the day is done
    Before I drift off to sleep, I check my phone
    Hoping for a message, a call, a tone
    That signifies your presence, your love so true
    I crave your voice, I miss us two
    I long to hear your laughter, your soothing words
    To feel connected, to fly with the birds
    In the sky so high, where we both belong
    Together forever, where nothing can go wrong
    Oh my dear, when will you be free
    To spend some time, just you and me
    To explore the world, hand in hand
    To make memories, to understand
    The depth of our love, the strength of our bond
    To create a life together, a magic beyond
    What words can express, what gestures can show
    The depth of my love to you, how much I know
    That you are my strength
    In this crazy world, you're always by my side
    So when we're apart, I feel lost and alone

THE HEALING POWER OF LOVE

Love is a balm
    To soothe the wounded soul
    A force that lifts the spirit
    To heights beyond control
    It shades the flaws and faults
    And sees the best in all
    Loving not for what one is
    But for who they are, beyond all
    The tears that stream in sorrow
    Are gently wiped away
    By hands that hold compassion
    And love that warms the day
    The smile that graces lips
    Is but a fraction of the joy
    That love brings to the heart
    And makes life worth a try

LONELINESS

Out in the world, surrounded by strangers
    I feel a sense of loneliness, a sense of danger
    I long for your company, your familiar touch
    But you are miles away, I miss you so much
    At work, you are busy, focused on the job
    Leaving me feeling isolated, feeling robbed
    Of precious moments together, of laughter and fun
    I count down the hours until the day is done
    Before I drift off to sleep, I check my phone
    Hoping for a message, a call, a tone
    That signifies your presence, your love so true
    I crave your voice, I miss us two
    I long to hear your laughter, your soothing words
    To feel connected, to fly with the birds
    In the sky so high, where we both belong
    Together forever, where nothing can go wrong
    Oh my dear, when will you be free
    To spend some time, just you and me
    To explore the world, hand in hand
    To make memories, to understand
    The depth of our love, the strength of our bond
    To create a life together, a magic beyond
    What words can express, what gestures can show
    The depth of my love to you, how much I know
    That you are my strength
    In this crazy world, you're always by my side
    So when we're apart, I feel lost and alone

But when we're together, my heart finds its home
I promise to wait, to be patient and kind
To cherish the moments we have, to bind
Our souls together, for eternity and more
I love you, my dear, to my very core

REFLECTIONS OF MATURITY

In the mirror, I see a reflection
    Of the person I used to be
    Yesterday, I was immature
    But today, I'm mature, can't you see
    I grew up when the world was simpler
    When things seemed to fall into place
    But now I find myself alone
    Wondering how I got here in this empty space
    If I were a boy, would things be different?
    Would I be seen and not ignored?
    But as a woman, I stand strong
    Even if no man sees me, I will not be floored
    For I am mature, I am grown
    And I will navigate this world on my own

TRUST IN TRANSITION

How can I believe in you
    Put my trust in what you say
    When you've betrayed me once before
    How can I know for sure
    That today you have turned
    From your deceitful ways
    How can I comprehend
    The words that you convey
    For you are like the weather
    Ever changing, ever gray

ECHOES OF TIME

In the still of night, darkness lingers on
    But morning arrives, bringing the light of dawn
    Minutes slip by and blend into hours
    As days merge into weeks with unseen powers
    Weeks fly by and swiftly turn to months
    As time weaves its way, defying confronts
    Months transform gracefully into years
    Amidst laughter, sorrow, and silent tears
Life's journey unfolds with each passing day
From the innocent child at play
Into adolescence, navigating the teenage years
Filled with hopes, dreams and unspoken fears
And then adulthood beckons with a steady hand
Challenging us to grow, to understand
The growth we experience, both inside and out
Navigating life's waters, amidst uncertainty and doubt
Through the twists and turns, highs and lows
We evolve and mature, as the river flows
From innocence to wisdom, we embark
On the ever-changing journey of life's grand arc

WOULD YOU LOVE ME NAKED?

When I strip away the layers
    Will you still desire me?
    Will you appreciate the imperfections
    The flaws that make me unique?
    Can you look beyond the façade
    And see the real me inside?
    Will you cherish my privacy
    And hold my truths with pride?
    For I am not just a false body
    I am more than meets the eye
    I long for your confession
    That you love me, faults and all, until we die.

FAMILY HUSTLE

This is our turn
    A family of hustlers we are
    Working hard, sweating under the harsh sun
    Cooking meals in wet places
    Searching for gold within dirty soils
    We have found against the cruel world
    Striving for a better life
    Now we are happier
    Proud of what we have achieved
    Together we bring the best to the table

WOULD YOU LOVE ME NAKED?

When I strip away the layers
    Will you still desire me?
    Will you appreciate the imperfections
    The flaws that make me unique?
    Can you look beyond the façade
    And see the real me inside?
    Will you cherish my privacy
    And hold my truths with pride?
    For I am not just a false body
    I am more than meets the eye
    I long for your confession
    That you love me, faults and all, until we die.

FAMILY HUSTLE

This is our turn
    A family of hustlers we are
    Working hard, sweating under the harsh sun
    Cooking meals in wet places
    Searching for gold within dirty soils
    We have found against the cruel world
    Striving for a better life
    Now we are happier
    Proud of what we have achieved
    Together we bring the best to the table

SOUL'S RESONANCE

In the depths of my soul
    I don't care what will happen
    For I know that God knows
    Whether I rest in peace or sadness
    I give my all to the world so cruel
    But I offer peace to mend
    To combine nations with love and faith
    As God intended me to be
    I trust that what I give
    Will surely come back to me
    For in spreading love and light
    I find true peace and harmony

PROMISE OF LOVE

If we take a break
    I would ask you one thing
    Think of yourself
    Make it clear in your mind
    That our love matters more
    Than your gang and friends
    I just want to make it clear
    As we are together
    Be the man of my dream
    And never let our love waver

ALONE IN THOUGHT

In silent room I lay
    Alone on my bed, a lonely way
    The feeling of aloneness deep within
    Though I chose this path, still a sting
    I see the happy couples around
    A twinge of envy, a silent sound
    But deep within, I know it's true
    This single life holds a beauty too
    The choice I made may feel so wrong
    When faced with love that goes along
    But in my heart, I must believe
    That this is my journey, my way to achieve
    In solitude, I'll find my peace
    And cherish the moments of just me
    Though sometimes the doubt creeps in
    I'll hold on to what I know within

LET'S BE FRIENDS

Let's be friends
    Enjoy the journey
    Together we soar
    Sharing laughs and more
    Believe in kindness
    Forgive and forget
    Rise above the negative
    Inspire each other
    Embrace diversity
    Empathy and love
    Never alone again
    Dreams become reality
    Hope for a better day
    Embrace the joy
    Resilience and strength
    Stay connected until the end

THE STRANGER

Stranger in the crowd
    Lost in the sea of faces
    Searching for a smile
    A connection, a warm embrace
    Eyes darting, looking for a sign
    In this world so vast and wide
    A stranger to some, but not to all
    There's kindness in every soul
    Reach out, make a friend
    For in the end, we're all the same
    In this world of strangers
    We find our own way
    In the midst of chaos
    There's a light that guides us
    A stranger no more
    For we are all connected
    In this journey of life
    Embracing the unknown
    With open hearts and minds

IMPERFECTLY PERFECT

I'm not just perfect, I am flawed
    A human being, learning from each fraud
    Life is short, no need to ponder
    Spread happiness, let doubts wander
    I believe in myself, success will applaud
    Rich in mind, poor in finances
    One day, I'll have both in trances
    Mistakes teach, growth is the key
    Imperfectly perfect, that's me
    I'll keep striving, taking chances

DEAR HAPPINESS

Dear happiness, we all need you, so
    We beg you to live with us, don't go
    In this cruel world, where selfishness rules
    The poor have long forgotten your jewels
    Fill their hearts with joy, make them glow

MY BEAUTIFUL MIND

I won't regret having you in my life
    The women of her own thoughts, so rife
    You are different from what people can think
    The pretty face with a beautiful mind, in sync
    Holding my success, you prove them wrong
    Beauty and brains, together we belong
    In a world that judges by appearance alone
    You shine brightly, like a gemstone
    Your intelligence matches your outer grace
    A rare combination, in this women race
    I won't regret the day we met
    For you are treasure, I'll never forget
    With you by my side, I feel complete
    In a world where true beauty is discreet

FADED LOVE

I used to love you deeply, once
    Heart entwined with yours, in dance
    But time, relentless, took its toll
    Leaving echoes of a love untold
    Now memories whisper, bittersweet
    Of a love that was once complete
    Faded slowly, like the evening sun
    Leaving shadows of what once began

LOST LOVE AT 3 AM

It was her arriving at 3 am, a sight that broke my heart
Where is she coming from, perhaps the cinema, or maybe the tavern?
The girl I used to love, now a dancer in the dark
She dances with other men when I'm not around
I can feel the distance between us, a chasm of despair
My hope for us dwindling with every passing hour
Her laughter is no longer mine to cherish
Her smile now a mask for a soul I no longer recognize
I remember the days of innocence, of love pure and true
But now she dances in shadows, a silhouette of our past
I watch from afar, a silent spectator in this tragic play
Her eyes no longer meet mine, avoiding the pain of my gaze
I wonder where it all went wrong, where our love lost its way
Was it the allure of the spotlight, the temptation of a new life?
Or was it my own failure to hold onto what we once had?
As the clock strikes 3 am, she disappears into the night
Leaving me alone with my shattered dreams and broken heart
It was her arriving at 3 am, a ghost of the girl I once knew
I am left to mourn the loss of the love we once shared

YOURS FOREVER

To be your close partner, now and ever
    Your favourite colour, I'll always wear
    The delicious food, I'll cook with care
    The music that delights you, I'll deliver
    Your smile, the sweetest sound I'll treasure
    I want to be solely yours, beyond compare
    In your heart, I aim to dwell, unaware
    Your love, my ultimate pleasure
    With every breath, I long to be near
    To hold your hand, to wipe your tears
    Your property, I'll gladly be yours
    My love for you, endless and pure

LET YOUR MAN LOVE YOU

Let your man love you, show interest, don't be shy
    To support, wake early, make him breakfast, try
    Provide for household, see love shining bright
    In return, his heart will be yours, day and night
    Embrace his passions, his dreams, encourage too
    Cherish his efforts, for what's real and true
    Love's not just words, but actions, clear and due
    Show him your care, let your love renew
    Let your man love you, in the little things
    In everyday moments, the joy it brings
    Support his endeavors, stand by his side
    Let your man love you, with unwavering pride

INNER STRUGGLE

I may say it's over, but deep down I know I don't mean
    Perhaps it's my anger, failing to control my emotions
    Oh dear, forgive me always, for being rude to you sometimes
    The battle within me, conflicts of heart and mind
    A storm rages within, a war of conflicting feelings
    I long for peace, yet turmoil reigns supreme
    In moments of anger, words uttered in haste
    Regret fills my heart, as I realize the damage done
    Please forgive me, my love, for the pain I've caused
    Let forgiveness be the bridge, to mend our broken bond
    I may say it's over, but deep down I know I don't mean
    For in my heart, you will always have a place
    A place of love, forgiveness and understanding
    Let us move forward, hand in hand, towards a brighter future
    Where anger and hurt are lessons learned, and love prevails in the end

DEAR MOM

Dear mom, your love embraced my early days
    In tender ways you soothed my childhood fears
    Your gentle hands, like angel's softest touch
    Guided my steps through laughter and through tears
    Dear mom, your wisdom shaped my growing mind
    Your words, a beacon in life's stormy sea
    Forever in my heart, your love I find
    A gift that's boundless, treasured endlessly

LOVE YOUR GIRL

For the true girl needs small things
    Just time to spend together
    Support her thoughts
    Even if she fails that judges
    Make her feel supported
    Don't let her down
    Because you won't find the same
    Don't cheat on her, stay true
    Cherish her, always be there
    In her laughter, in her tears
    Hold her close, never let go
    Love her endlessly, let her know
    For a girl's heart is fragile
    Handle with care, be gentle
    For in your love, she'll bloom
    In your absence, she'll gloom
    So hold her hand, walk by her side
    In love and faith, let her guide

FOREVER IN 24 HOURS

Within 24 hours we spend so close
    Babe is it 24/7 that we chose
    Together we are, inseparable as one
    Babe you know you are my shining sun
    With each passing minute, my love grows
    In your arms, my heart forever flows
    The clock ticks on, but time stands still
    In your presence, I find my fill
    Cherishing every moment we share
    Knowing that you'll always be there
    Within 24 hours, my world is complete
    With you by my side, my heart skips a beat

LOST IN THE DREAM

The dream came through the mind in the cool darkness

Do I still remember it, or is it just a dream they say?

How could she appear in my lost mind, with a smile trying to hold my hand?

By the time I tried to catch up, my mind lost in the darkness

The real one comes to break what I saw

Leaving me wondering if it was all just a dream

Lost in the dream, I search for her smile

But it fades away like a fleeting shadow

In the depths of my mind

She remains a mystery, a figment of my imagination

The dream came and went

Leaving me with unanswered questions

Lost in the darkness of my own thoughts

THE WORLD MUST KNOW

The world must know the beauty of being together
    Or should it see me and you as one through its eyes
    How we have built this compound that is insoluble
    Never reacting with other elements as we harmonize
    It must learn from our experience of love and care
    Embracing the bond we share so rare and true
    Let it witness the strength of our unity
    And how we weather storms as one entity
    For in our togetherness lies the secret
    Of peace, understanding, and unwavering support
    The world must see us as an example
    Of how love conquer all obstacles and distort

SELF-REFLECTION

I always ask myself, am I shy
    Do others see me in that light, they say?
    Yet when alone, my thoughts do not shy away
    Engaging in conversations that never die
    I ponder if it's true, what they portray
    Perhaps they see me differently than I
    Maybe it's the way I talk to just one guy
    Not realizing how it may look from far away
    But deep down, I know the truth lies
    I speak to myself to find the answers
    Seeking solace in my own company
    While others may judge with critical eyes
    Yet in my solitude, I am the master
    Of my thoughts, my words, and my symphony

BEAUTY UNMATCHED

Since I met you, I've come to see
    That thinking flowers pale in comparison to thee
    I once believed they were the most beautiful sight
    But in your presence, they fade like night
    Your beauty surpasses anything in bloom
    Your radiance pierces through the gloom
    The leaves that change their hues in the fall
    Cannot match the colours you enthral
    Your own hue, unique and divine
    Outshines all nature's design
    The stems that hold the petals high
    Are but a shadow when you pass by
    Your body, a masterpiece of grace
    In which all beauty finds its place
    I was wrong to think flowers held the key
    For in you, I find true beauty
    Unmatched by any tree

STRUGGLING WITH LOVE

I may think of myself, why must I let go
    Is it not better to hold on through the pain?
    To face the challenges and grow
    And strive to love again
    Perhaps as a man, I must stand strong
    But what if being hurt is the test?
    I try to love, but is it wrong
    To hold back and protect myself from the rest
    Do I need to give my heart away
    Before I can truly find love?
    Or is it better to wait and stray
    From the path that overwhelms me like a dove
    These questions linger in my mind
    As I navigate this journey, searching for what I may find

IN THE QUIET OF NIHGT

In the quiet of night
    The stars whisper softly
    Their ancient tales unfold
    To light the earth below
    And the domestic animals
    Gather close, steadfast
    To provide for a man
    In the circle of life
    The years turn slowly
    My age catches up
    Yet still, I seek
    To find you
    The safest place
    Close to me
    I can't let you cry, dear
    Without you
    I will be lost
    In the darkest road
    What could I be
    In this world so cruel
    Maybe a good seed
    Planted on dry land
    Failing to get water
    To germinate
    Hope springs eternal
    In the heart's quiet depths
    Love, a guiding star

Through life's winding paths
The stars above
Continue their dance
Watching over us
In the quiet of night

UNSPOKEN SECRETS

Within the heart
    Deep inside
    There are the words unspoken
    The words kept for strangers or enemies
    They're called 'secrets'
    Maybe they are special
    Because they keep big insides
    Even dangerous things are held for unknown
    A hidden treasure
    A silent power
    Kept safe within
    A fortress of emotion
    Guarded by silence
    Whispers of truth
    Echo in the chambers
    Of the heart
    A sacred space
    Where secrets reside
    Untouched by time
    Hidden from sight
    Forever safe
    In the depths of the soul

THE CHANGING WORLD

The powers of men they used to hold dear
    In families, they were honoured with respect
    But now the tides have turned, it's clear
    No longer do they stand as heads, unchecked
    The laws have spoken, preaching equality
    But do they truly seek to level the playing field?
    Or merely test men's capabilities
    And see if they will bend or if they'll yield?
    No more cheating, fairness must prevail
    For in this changing world, we must adapt
    Embrace the shift, and let old customs fail
    No longer do we turn a blind eye, accept
    The world may change, but men must rise
    To meet the challenge, see with new eyes

THE STRENGTH OF THE FAMILY

The family, a treasure trove of love and care
    Molding man's thinking with each passing day
    Through support and guidance, success is made fair
    Their presence, a shield against dismay
    United by blood, a bond unbreakable and true
    Each member a piece of a priceless puzzle
    Their loyalty unwavering, through and through
    A force that no adversity can muzzle
    Blood is thinker than water, so they say
    A truth proven time and time again
    In times of trials, they light the way
    A source of strength, a harbour in the rain

THE DIFFICULT ROAD OF LOVE

I may feel sorry in my mind, to judge over the distance
    Over the married couples, maybe I'm wrong who knows
    But opinions I hold still, for I have the feelings as a person
    That love to marriage is the difficult road
    But is it what I believe, or just observations I made
    Love in marriage needs serious dedication, it's true
    To navigate the highs and lows, the joy and pain
    To weather the storm and dance in the rain
    It takes strength and courage, a heart that's willing
    To put in the work, to keep the love fulfilling
    To forgive and forget, to compromise and adapt
    To embrace the flaws, the imperfections, and still be glad
    So I may feel sorry for those on this path
    But deep down I know, it's a journey worth the wrath
    For in the end, it's the love that remains
    A bond that transcends, a connection that sustains
    So let me not judge, but offer my support
    For love in marriage is not easy, but it's worth the effort
    To grow together, to build a life as one
    To face the challenges and still have fun
    Here's to love in marriage, may it always endure
    May it be a beacon of hope, a light pure
    For in the end, it's the love that we cherish
    A bond so strong, that no distance can perish

ENCOUNTER

It was last afternoon
    The time, I guess, was 2 to 1 hour before sunset
    I was focusing on my way
    But you disturbed my mind
    How should I pass by
    Leaving so attractive person moving alone on the street?
    I did greet you 'hi'
    But your smile just answered me
    You were so amazing
    Since I met you
    You never been angry to anything
    You always give a smile to anybody

NEVER BEG FOR LOVE

Never beg someone to be in your life
    If they don't show up, just leave
    Ignoring texts, calls, and messages
    Value yourself, that's key
    Don't chase after empty promises
    Or cling to someone who doesn't care
    You deserve more than half-hearted love
    Never settle for what isn't there
    Know your worth and stand tall
    Don't beg for someone to stay
    If they can't see your value
    It's time to walk away
    Love should be freely given
    Not forced or begged for in vain
    Respect yourself enough to know
    You shouldn't have to explain
    Don't lower your standards
    Just to keep someone around
    True love will come to you
    When the right person is found

RENEWAL

Fresh and young in days of endless time
    But failing to think with clarity's chime
    To hold on to important things I stray
    Ignoring what should guide my way
    Just interested in fleeting uses found
    The happiness once, in shallow ground
    Rather than focusing on what's ahead
    Oh, God, change my mind, where dreams are led
    Renew it, let it focus, understand
    The world behind, its truths so grand

DREAM OF A KISS

Once upon a kiss, the world stood still
    Two souls entwined in a dance of desire
    Lips meeting in a sweet, stolen thrill
    A moment of pure passion, set on fire
    In that fleeting touch, time ceased to exist
    Hearts racing, a symphony of bliss
    In the silence, whispers of love were heard
    A connection deeper than any word
    Eyes locked, telling tales untold

A HEART'S GRATITUDE

I remember when we first started talking
    You were the first person to put a real smile on my face
    In a long time
    You're the reason I go to bed and wake up with a smile
    I want to thank you for just being you
    And I want you to know that
    I have fallen deeply in love with you
    Love you, babe

THE BOND THAT ENDURES

In the darkness of night
    Our bond shines bright
    Like a golden stone
    You're my power, my own
    Without you, I'd be lost
    In a world so cold and frost
    The love we share endures
    In our hearts, forever secure

OCEAN SERENITY

It was just you and me
    Beside the waters
    From ocean view
    The light rays from above
    Warm up our cool bodies
    The soft sound comes by
    Making our happiness
    Oh, with you
    My life is so much better
    Because I know you're there for me
    Whenever I'm lost in the sea
    Your caring heart guides me
    Love like the ocean deep
    Our souls forever intertwined
    In this blissful eternity
    Together in love's embrace
    In this picturesque scene
    Our heart beat as one
    Under the guidance of the moon

About the Author

Matlotlo Sejake is an accomplished poet whose evocative verses delve deep into the intricate tapestry of human emotions. Following the success of his debut poetry collection, 'Verses of the Soul' (October 2023), which eloquently explores themes of emotions, sorrow, nature, and animals, Sejake returns with 'Love's Spectrum: bliss to Heartache.' This second anthology delves into the complexities of love, from moments of ecstatic bliss to profound experiences of heartache. With a keen eye for detail and a lyrical voice that resonates with authenticity, Sejake continues to captivate readers with his poetic exploration of love's emotional spectrum.

Milton Keynes UK
Ingram Content Group UK Ltd.
UKHW030700170824
447045UK00001B/18